My Garden
&
Other Poems

by
Mike Hamill

My Garden & Other Poems

Author: Mike Hamill

Copyright © 2025 Mike Hamill

The right of Mike Hamill to be identified as author of this work has been asserted by the author in accordance with section 77 and 78 of the Copyright, Designs and Patents Act 1988.

ISBN 978-1-83538-514-2 (Paperback)
      978-1-83538-515-9 (E-Book)

Cover Design and Book Layout by:
    Maple Publishers
    www.maplepublishers.com

Published by:
    Maple Publishers
    Fairbourne Drive, Atterbury,
    Milton Keynes,
    MK10 9RG, UK
    www.maplepublishers.com

A CIP catalogue record for this title is available from the British Library.
All rights reserved. No part of this book may be reproduced or translated by any form or by any means, electronic or mechanical, including photocopying, recording or by any information storage and retrieval system without written permission from the author.
The views expressed in this work are solely those of the author and do not necessarily reflect the views of the publisher, and the publisher hereby disclaims any responsibility for them.

I'd like to thank the folks at Maple publishing for making this process possible. There is a special mention to Isha, who has held my hand throughout the process and borne my occasional last minute changes with remarkable good grace.

Also, thanks goes to the encouragement of friends and family to publish my words, with special mention to Peter and Sue Brumlik— friends and mentors.

Finally, this book is dedicated to the memory of my wife, Audrey.

Contents

Anthology 9

My Garden 10

Dream Not of Today 11

Alone In Flanders No More 12

Old Men 13

The Fallen 14

In A Foreign Field 15

Normandy 6th June 17

The Guns Fall Silent 19

Bluff Cove 20

Remembrance 2020 21

Silence 22

The Longest March 23

D Day 24

The Rescue 26

Lost Family 28

The Chicken & The Egg 29

The Nose 30

Beneath The Sea 31

A Seal 32

The Colliwob 33

Sid the Snake 35

The Compost Heap	37
Jack The Arachnoid	38
The Frou- Frou Bird	39
Good Morning	40
The Animal Games	41
A Cat In A Hat	43
The Dance	44
Winston	45
The Monkey and The Kangaroo	47
The Forest Faerie	48
The Mouse	49
The Goat	50
The Heffalump	51
Hedge The Hedgehog	52
The Buffoon	53
Georgie	54
The Question Resolved	55
The Purple Crane	56
Pretty Boy	57
The Dragonfly	58
A Purple Road	59
Octopussy	61
Quentin The Caterpillar	63
The Storm	64

The Coral Steps	65
Jack in London	67
Morning	68
The Day	69
Nighttime Dreams	70
Mountainsides	71
The Autumn	73
The Journey	75
Perfect Lines	76
Shapes	78
Goodnight Mama	79
Another Springtime Day	80
Consternation	81
Can You See?	82
Dawn Breaks	83
Destitution	84
Dreams	85
Evening Scenes	86
Endless nights	87
Lost Memories	89
Good Night	90
Hands Touch	91
Mother, Maiden & Crone	92
Light over Dark	93

My Eyes Are Closed	94
My New Sisters	95
Old Age Is No Fun	96
The Kiss	98
Nature	99
Requiem For Nigel	100
Cake	101
Shadows	102
Pain	103
Solitude	104
Starlings	105
The Stars	106
Summertime	107
Tenements	108
The Birds	109
The Fading Sun	110
The Garden	111
I Touch	112
The Moon	113
The Dance	114
The River	115
The Stream	116
The Train	117
The Wind	118

Twilight	120
The Starlight	121
Spring	122
Valhalla	123
A Winter Morning	124
It's 2 AM	125
The Nighttime	127
Will-o'-the-Wisp	128
Dappled Glades	129
On The Beach	130
Whispers	131
The Rainbow Bridge	132
Moonbeams And Raindrops	133
Her Majesty's Farewell	134
A Hebridean Sky	135
Icicles	136
Pathways	137
Broken Dreams	138
Another Winter's Tale	139
Winters Mist	140
Friends	141
Table For One	143
The Last Hurrah	144

Anthology

This book is of words from my heart,
written from my soul; in part.
I regained the will to pick up the pen
and enjoyed my writing, once again!
This reflects the joy and pain that I've had
some are good and some quite bad!
I hope you enjoy without the distractions,
of misspelling or grammar infractions.

December 2024

Mike Hamill

My Garden

I love my little garden, the places where I sit,
In quiet contemplation. I love it, every bit.
The Acer trees in red, and golden copper hues,
the agapanthus, in shades of glorious blue.

The peace the of Buddha's.
The tranquillity that they bring.
The visiting of songbirds. Oh my, can they sing.
The warriors on guard, protecting all they see.
The peace and serenity that's all around me.

And, on the garden bench, near where my lady lies.
I oft sit in reflection, as tears still fill my eyes.
Or, in a summers soft evening light,
to sit and watch the lights glow, till draws in the night.

My garden is my guardian. It's protection never ends.
And, for a time, normality it transcends.
So, welcome to my garden; my place on this sweet earth.
My oasis of tranquillity. My garden. My Garth.

Dream Not of Today

Close your eyes but dream not of today.
But let your mind wander, tumble, and stray,
to a time past, when youth were bold,
left their homes. Some, to never grow old.

Listen with open ears to the steady drumbeat,
the sound of warriors marching feet.
Catch the sun glistening in fields of red,
where poppies grow in the fallen's stead.

Breathe deeply. Taste the fog of war,
and the warriors lost for evermore.
Those who answered the bugle call.
Who stood side by side, upright and tall.

Let your heart swell with utmost pride,
at the giants who, with measured stride,
walked into danger. Some never to return.
No braver accolades did they earn.

It is for us to stand, foursquare as one
and face the evenings setting sun.
At parade, Cenotaph or Arboretum,
we say, with pride. We will remember them.

Mike Hamill

Alone In Flanders No More

You've laid alone all these years.
No one to stand over you, shed their tears.
You have been lost, in a field.
But now, from that place, you are revealed.
No longer one of those missing souls,
whose name is engraved in remembrance rolls.
But now you are found; no longer alone.
Lying with Brethren neath Regimental stone.
Rest in peace brave soldier. We owe a debt
You gave your tomorrow. We will never forget

Old Men

The old men gather between hallowed walls,
On village greens and in lofty grandeured halls.
They speak in whispers, their eyes and voices dim
They meet with comrades, friends, each one a pilgrim.
There was laughter and banter 'tween opposing groups,
Individually they carried their colours; but together they were troops.
Boys to men, they'd come of age when needed by their land,
Marching proudly; behind their chosen band.
And now these men, with bodies bent, all answer a greater call.
For men and women no longer here. But family all.
To come together, to remember the cause.
The men in scarlet lead, to echoing applause
And then, came the quiet command, "Parade!"
And bent backs and broken limbs each, an effort made.
Standing tall and straight, a tear falls here and there
But everyone there that day, did their poppy proudly wear.
As they remembered, those who no longer live.
But gave us everything, that they had left to give.

Mike Hamill

The Fallen

We are the fallen. Who hears our cries?
No breath remaining, no lasting sighs
Those who loved us joined in grief.
only in their hearts lives the belief.

We are the fallen, we march in eternity.
Once 'twas them and us, but now just we
Kindred souls, comrades at last.
Joined by the memories of battles past.

We are the fallen, but not all of us lie
Under the soil or monument high.
We still stand though. The battles remain,
And we, broken in body and the mind in pain

We are the fallen, in some foreign field
Our bodies never found, never revealed
But we are there together, in unity
As you stand proud. And remember me.

In A Foreign Field

The thunder rolls across the valley,
as lightning strikes a grey stone Abbey.
The dark clouds boil in the menacing sky,
as daylight fails and passes by.
To be replaced by the other thunder,
that tears a life. Full asunder.

And, in the distance; more flashes bloom.
Armageddon? It is coming soon.
Nature's fury, fierce at best,
is subdued by the unwavering quest
to rain upon their fellow men,
nightmares and destruction, again and again

And, in trenches, slits and holes,
brave folk cower and pray for souls.
In fields of stinking, cloying mud,
and draining of a warrior's blood.
But no respite, for man nor, beast.
As, yet another life has ceased.

Mike Hamill

The vista that is displayed,
Of shattered trees, stripped and flayed.
Of each, in the muddy polyandrium consigned.
Lost forever, except in heart and mind.
Of men and women, who we thank.
Who paid in full at life's bank.

And those who returned incomplete
and march to a muffled beat.
With broken bones. No limbs or sight,
and visited by demons. Day and night.
Hold your heads up high and tall
As we who live, thank you all.

Normandy 6th June

The skies lighten and they face the dawn.
See the faces, haggard and drawn.
The dark turgid waters. The grey icing spray
Heralds the start of the momentous day.

Soldiers gather in nervous throng
All comrades. All belong.
Families, regiments, battalions, brigades.
Friendly rivalries to the side are laid.

Sailors work and ready the guns,
hooded in white. Ghostly apparitions
The boats are lowered and sent away.
On this, the most dreadful day.

In the skies, high above in waves they come.
Father's, brothers. Someone's precious son.
Heading for Pegasus to hold till relieved.
Oh, the bravery to be believed.

And now from the sea the thunder rolls
And, on the shore, the horrors unfold
As men; some just children yesterday
Witness deaths evil bouquet.

They fought with passion; their fear contained.
But in their hearts, it remained.
Amongst the bodies some old friends
Some injuries heal. Others never mend.

And now the survivors land once more,
On that French, foreign shore.
Old men, women, the last time they'll gather.
But we will remember them. Forever.

The Guns Fall Silent

11 AM, the guns fall silent and the thunder stills.
Just the cries of the wounded, the emptiness fills!
Is it over? Does the fighting end,
can we now our weary way, homeward wend?
Home to our families, our children, our kin?
Can we smile now; would it be a sin?
We are the lucky ones, or so they say,
to have made it, to this auspicious day.
But there are those still broken, in body and mind.
Some whose injuries. they'll never find!
And those who have fallen, forever concealed,
beneath the soil, in a foreign field.
They gave us everything, their life, their youth.
And we will respect them, in honour and truth.
So, stand tall, as the words you humbly say!
For our tomorrow's, they gave their today
We will remember them!

Mike Hamill

Bluff Cove

I stood on those cliffs and through closed eyes what did I see?
The Galahad there, rolling in the waves, broken and free.
The cries of the men drift over me, in screaming pain,
and the rescuers return, again and again.

I see them now on Bluff Coves towering slopes,
the broken soldiers and sailors. Just blokes!
I hear their voices where now seagulls cry,
I see the bodies of those who die.

I stand on those cliffs and see, in my mind's eye,
those who's souls stayed beneath the dark, dark sky.
In the oceans cold water their bodies will lie
and I see their souls, endlessly, go marching by.

Remembrance 2020

There is no sound, but we know they are there.
The silence comes loudly, in whispering prayer
The feet in cadence, march a measured pace.
With heads held high, in perpetual grace.

Can you hear the silence, does it fill your mind
Are their heartbeats, with yours entwined?
Can you hear them sing Tipperary. Over and over
Or even the words of the White Cliffs of Dover?

Will you recall those that laid down their lives.
And those, with injuries, who still survive.
Listen carefully, no warriors will condemn
As you lift your hearts and repeat.
We will remember them.

Silence

They marched in silence, their heads held high,
not seen by the thousands standing by.
They marched with friends, comrades all.
They marched like when they took the call.
They marched with those from yesterday, in sorrow,
for they cannot march with those of tomorrow.
Their eyes see only long-gone scenes,
they only hear the battle screams.
They would be old, but they march as youth.
What they were once, 'tis the truth!
They walk as men and women too,
Brave? No, just folk like me and you.
So, when you stand on Remembrance Day,
heads bowed and you softly say.
"You have come from close by and faraway
but please; can I march with you today?"
You gave everything you had to give
so that we in harmony could live.
So come with us as we observe
with honour, those that gave and served.

My Garden & Other Poems

The Longest March

I stood amongst a sea of faces,
each one riven from different places.
They walked together on tired feet,
driven by the slow drumbeat.
Arms linked in quiet progression,
transported in a slow procession,
heads bowed in fearful convocation,
shared sorrow and supplication.
The concourse ready to greet their fears,
that lie amongst the falling tears.
The daylight fades, the journey end.
And the faces? Into darkness blend!

Mike Hamill

D Day

The dawn comes slowly. A guarded light
As Sword and Gold come into sight.
Men huddle in corridors and companionway
Some talk quietly, others pray.

Sandwiches shared. Tea is brewed
Cigarettes smoked. The air is blue
Above, the Airborne fly on by.
The RAF protect, from low to high.

The crash of the waves, and the Naval gun.
The desire to live. To run, run run.
Through the surf, up the beach
Sanctuary, safety, I must reach.

Comrades fall like broken mannequins
As men swim in desperation
The ripping sounds as bullets slash
And you know how closely they have passed.

The day continues long and hard
We advance. Yard by yard
Positions taken slowly, up the beach.
Till at last the objectives, finally reached.

Now we rest our heads and catch our breath
And find remorse at all the death.
And we lift our heads and softly pray,
to give thanks, that we've survived, D Day.

Those brave and wonderous men who gave their all
Some to remain where they fall!
Their sacrifice that we could live.
Some gave all that they could give.

We Will Remember Them.

Mike Hamill

The Rescue

The dark night crashes down, and shadows chase.
The wind kicks spume deep in my face.
I rise and fall and spin, as I keep
my body from dying in the deep.

The lightning flashes over the boiling seas,
The wind screams, 'tis no summer breeze.
The wild cursed sea turns to darkest black,
The winds bowl in, in a counterattack!

The moment nears, I cry in despair,
will soon I lie in Neptune's lair?
Will those demons draw me to the deep,
will I forever, in the cold depths sleep?

My head is filled with a muted beat
my eyes to the heavens rise to seek
A star above is shining bright
it glows through the stormy, raging night.

The midnight sun grows brighter still,
and my ears with heavenly words do fill.
An angel appears, bright in this endless dark sea!
smiles and says, "hello mate. home for tea?"

And within the angels' arms I am embraced.
We rise and the cruel seas are chased.
Now gathered in its welcome womb,
my rescue helicopter does homeward zoom

Mike Hamill

Lost Family

We may not know them. But they are family.
Siblings, born of the military.
Brothers and Sisters who have lived a life,
shared comradeship, in laughter and strife.
Done things, that not many have achieved.
Told wild tales. Some even believed!
And, when they depart, for a safer place; we can raise a glass to one another,
and bid a military farewell, to each lost Sister, or Brother.

The Chicken & The Egg

It was just the other day,
whilst I was on my way,
to visit with old Crimkin
I came upon a chicken.
I asked her, for she was she,
if she would lay an egg for me?
She gave a cluck, and shook each leg,
and produced a quintessential cubic egg.
It was so perfect, so bourgeoisie.
I took it home, just for my tea.

Mike Hamill

The Nose

There was an individual, named Old Joe,
whose nose required an occasional blow!
His proboscis was large, a bit of a brute,
and his nasal passages; immensely hirsute.
When forewarned by a light, tickling sensation,
he would make all necessary preparation.
He'd take his red hankie, 'twas never blue,
and blow his conk, through and through.
And then, upon reflection he would find,
wonders of almost every kind!
The occasional cat, a few grunting pigs,
a rat and once, a bundle of twigs!
But, the most amazing thing, to which I now refer,
was the emergence of the neighbour's, Combine Harvester.
Joe now suffers some strange old ails
as all his sneezes come out in bales!

Beneath The Sea

I looked upon an iridescent sea
and saw an octopus wave at me.
It opened out its eight long arms,
encompassing me in loving charms.
From above, the bright and sliding skies,
mesmerised me with smoke filled pyres.
A golden mermaid, on a turtle's leather back
smiled at me 'neath her silk yashmak.
And called to me like the Lorelei
and pulled me into her silvered eye.
And there, I found the whitest whale,
who told to me an intoxicating tale.
Of lands and sights in oceans deep.
Of kingly battles, where princesses weep.
Where dolphins chase, and seahorses gallop
And children play tiddlywinks with a scallop.
All this and more, I did see.
Beneath the waves, beneath the sea

Mike Hamill

A Seal

I saw a seal with a ginger beard,
his hair was green; it was so weird.
He wore a suit of midnight blue,
I tell you this and it's so true!

He walked a distance in his slippers
They fitted nicely, on his flippers!
He smiled and doffed his hat to you,
and joined the waiting taxi queue.

Take me to the sea my man,
And make it snappy, if you can?
They went so fast at quite a clip,
And Seal left driver, a herring as a tip.

He walked right down to the beach
And, as the sea he did reach,
he turned and gave a little nod.
And into the water he did plod.

He swam away, into the night,
and ate a whale for his appetite.
He burped a lot and gave a trump.
And onto the beach, three boats were dumped!

The Colliwob

The Colliwob is a curious beast,
it's got shaggy hair and has sharp teeth.
It has a very peculiar face,
as nothings quite in the right place.

It has a horn upon its head
that's not quite purple; but dark and red.
It has a foot that has ten toes!
For what reason, no one knows?

It has three ears so it can hear,
two at the side, one at the rear,
eyes it has but again there's three.
One looks back to where it's been you see!

It has a sort of shuffling gait,
that kind of weird and so ornate.
Two steps forward, one step back.
And a hop, skip and jump to stay on track!

Its nose? It is a peculiar orifice,
green and completely ambidextrous!
Its four-foot tall and six foot wide,
you'd think it could not really hide?

Mike Hamill

But you'll not see the Colliwob.
This strange and mystical thingmabob!
But it has my utmost admiration,
as it lives deep, inside my imagination?

Sid the Snake

The mouse looked across waters of Green and Blue
and heard a hissing voice call! Hello; Yoo-hoo!
He looked behind a passing boat; and there, in its wake.
He saw a long and wriggling, multi-coloured snake.

It spoke again in a quiet voice, and bid
a soft hello. How do you do? My name's Sid!
To Mouse's side he quickly went, and too his big surprise
slithered up and around him and looked into his eyes!

Mouse saw one eye was red and the other black.
and Sid had yellow spots arranged upon his back!
He had a mouth which he opened wide
and there were lots of teeth, glistening inside!

He flicked his tongue and said in mouse's ear
oooh, you taste so sweet. Come for tea my dear!
He seemed so nice that the mouse said yes
He would be pleased to come for tea; and be his guest.

Sid hissed softly and said the pleasure'ssss mine
and led mouse off to his house where he would dine!
At the house, Sid stood by and opened the door
Mouse skipped in joyfully and then; was seen no more!

Mike Hamill

So, if you meet a long and wriggly coloured snake,
don't be like mouse and make a big mistake.
If Sid invites you to his house for a bite to eat.
Say no and go! Before in his sandwich, you are the meat!

The Compost Heap

I saw a worm once 'twas a wriggling thing?
But, oh my, my, it could sing.
It lived inside the compost heap
And would, on occasion, take a peep.
I saw it one night in bow tie and tails,
surrounded by an orchestra of snails!
I stood there quietly, all aquiver!
And, as it sang; I felt a shiver.
It sang with gusto and panache.
With tears my eyes were all awash.
What a star it was, such a performer
as it belted out Nessun Dorma!

Mike Hamill

Jack The Arachnoid

There once was a spider. I'll call him Jack.
He had loads of eyes and hairs on his back!
He resided neath the stereo; quite peacefully
And now and again he'd pops out, to say hi to me.
Now I don't like spiders, they are creepy, not fun,
So, I thought long and hard how to make him run!
The horse chestnut, it seems, isn't their favourite scent
It causes distress and they do dement!
So, I surrounded his hideaway with conkers you see
But still, he comes out and just laughs at me!

The Frou- Frou Bird

Down on the coast beside the sea,
in Norfolk land, there lives for free,
a creature of great stature see!
It is the pride of the animal bourgeoisie.
The creatures' tall and five-foot-wide
It has a mouth! But no teeth inside!
Upon the water, it makes a mark
as in the darkness it does park.
It floats with decorum, belly up.
And on its tum, there rests a cup,
filled with milk and hot clementine
And on the side, a slice of lime.
The frou-frou bird, a strange nomenclature,
but, oh, such an adventurer
Opens a flap within its derriere,
and spreads a sail to catch some air
And with a jovial wave of its liquorice crutch
shouts goodbye; thanks very much.
It turns and paddles slowly, out to sea.
To hunt for snarkpuffs for its tea!

Mike Hamill

Good Morning

Good morning, good morning, the cockerel cries.
As he raises his comb to the nights demise.
Good morning, good morning, hear the milkmaids' hails.
As they leave the barn with brimming pails!
Good morning, good morning cries the cook midst her clutter,
Spreading toast with jam and butter.
Good morning, the children cry from the kitchen stool,
Soon they'll be off for a day at school.
Good morning grumbles the Master with a worried frown.
Off to do business in the local town.
And the Mistress? Well, with barely a peep,
She rolls right over and goes back to sleep.

The Animal Games

Today, I played leapfrog with a toad.
It was an uplifting experience, I'll be blowed.
We leapt around the lake, from shore to shore.
And, at the end toad said; let's play some more?
He leapt onto a lily pad in the middle of the lake.
A running jump, I then did take!
Alas, my leap was short, and I didn't get
to join toad upon the pad. I just got wet!

I played tag today, with a lovely dragonfly
it shouted you're it, as it floated by.
And then, by the winds' softest breath
It flew so high. And it just left!
Now, this was hard, how could it be,
I would be it; permanently!
I looked around and began to cry,
there was no sign of the dragonfly!

With a Chameleon, I played hide and seek.
I closed my eyes and did not peek.
I counted down, from ten to one
and when I looked, she was gone!
I searched for her just high and low
and know not where she did go?

Mike Hamill

And then, her eyelids opened, and I could see
She'd just been sitting there, upon my knee

Today I played hopscotch with a kangaroo.
Just a baby one, it was true!
But he did the lot in two short bounds
and won each of the remaining rounds!
He laughed, and said, go on mate,
take a turn! I can wait.
I was not happy, I became a grouch
Kanga just smiled and popped into his mama's pouch

A Cat In A Hat

There was a cat, who thought that,
it was indeed much better than that!
So much so he bought a hat.
Oh, he's such an important cat!

He walked about in the lounge,
tail erect he strolled around.
And, in the mirror himself he did espy.
And thought, what a great cat am I?

Into the garden he then paraded,
and the self-importance has pervaded,
and other homes he then invaded.
He just could not be dissuaded!

The other cats did vociferously cry,
what have we here? Oh my, Oh my!
A cat in a hat? It's just not true,
how silly; and non-feline are you?

So, he retired back to his bed,
and removed the hat from upon his head!
He fell asleep to dream of things, that are just cat.
Birds, mice and toys. But never, ever again; a hat!

Mike Hamill

The Dance

Last night I had a dance with an EliTig
It was huge, Oh so big.
We danced a waltz, a foxtrot too.
It left no footprint in the morning dew.
It did, on occasion, burst into song,
and showed me, its polka dotted thong.
I loved my dance with the EliTig,
'twas just the perfect late-night gig.
But alas, as the morning came once more,
and EliTig walked out the door.
My bedroom I could clearly see.
And it looked completely wrecked to me.
The bedside lamp was on the floor,
my little clock outside the door.
My spectacles? Well, nuff said.
I found them behind the bed!
So, there's a motto here you see.
And to you, I pass it on for free.
Next time you want a nighttime dance.
Don't give the EliTig a single glance

Winston

I saw a thing upon a hill,
It wasn't well, it looks quite ill.
It has no legs but did have flippers
and a beak, like a pair of wire strippers.

It flapped its wing, for it had but one.
When it's one hundred, the other will come.
It opened its colourful, pinkish beak,
and with a trill began to speak.

"Ow do cocker," it said to me,
In an accent that was pure estuary.
He carefully stroked his blue goatee,
and said, "shall we partake of marmalade tea?"

He poured from the cup to his yellow teapot,
and never spilt a single drop.
He looked at me with a twinkling smile,
and said, "'elp yourself, stay awhile."

So, I took a slice of humble pie
and had a drink! Oh my, oh my.
I said to my host, who besides me stood,
"Winston mate, that's very good!"

Mike Hamill

He gently smiled with his pinkish beak,
and gave his green 'tash a little tweak.
And said, "that's good, the pleasure's mine
now, would you like some dangberry wine?"

I took a glass, just to be polite,
raised it and took a little bite.
And then there was the loudest crash.
and Winston disappeared, in a flash.

The Monkey and The Kangaroo

Today, the Monkey and the Kangaroo,
decided to spend the day at the local zoo.
They planned on a picnic, their favourite thing.
They pondered long and hard, what to bring?
Monkey had nuts, fruit, honey, and wine
Kanga had leaves and shoots. He'd be chewing some time!
They walked into the zoo hand in hand,
their tails dragging gently, in the sand.
They stood amazed at the creatures there
And wandered, just about everywhere.
They had their picnic in the park,
and, nearby, saw a warthog family, have a lark!
Mother Warthog had cooked up a feast,
of insects, worms, and something deceased!
Father Warthog had a satisfying wallow.
And, on occasion, at the kids, he would bellow
Kanga and Monkey, continued their ambulation
and, finally, on contemplation,
thought that the day had been a big success.
Kanga asked Monkey which exhibit was best?
Monkey looked pensive and thought for a while.
Then said. "Why Kanga, the humans, by a mile"

Mike Hamill

The Forest Faerie

Upon a yellow toadstool there sits such a sight,
in a pink, frilly romper suit. Shiny and bright.
The forest fairy smiles, such a happy grin.
It mesmerises me, and slowly draws me in.
Her smile is beguiling, beneath her tartan hair.
As slowly, she peels, a giant purple pear.
Beside her on the toadstool, sits her elephant.
Reclining quite nicely, beside her turquoise tent!
She Pirouettes quite gracefully, dressed in a pink tutu.
While dancing to My Generation, by the band The Who.
The forest fairy smiles and gently wipes each lip
And, oh so softly, she quietly does quip.
It's been so nice to meet you.
I'm off now, toodle-oo.

The Mouse

In some dusty corner of my house
There reigns supreme, a little mouse.
I've not seen him, or her, in the flesh.
But I've heard the sound, a soft caress.
As round the skirting it does roam,
and make itself so at home!
It has at my expense,
nicked my food! I am incensed.
It wanders off to digest,
and, round the house, leaves a mess.
Now, I'm not one to cause a fuss!
But it's time it was leaving us!
I asked it kindly to take its leave,
but it gave me no reprieve.
So, I baited a springy trap!
Guess what happened? It went snap!
At last, I thought it's now done, I am rid.
Except, now I'm uncle to her kid!

Mike Hamill

The Goat

I saw the sky 'twas pink and green,
the funniest thing that I've ever seen.
And then, there upon a yellow hill.
A purple crow gave a trill.
An orange cloud went floating by,
whilst a woolly goat, gave a sigh.
It's never good, I heard him bleat,
when it itches, on my feet!
But, I suppose, it would be much less fun,
if the itch, was upon my bum!

The Heffalump

The Heffalump is a beautiful creature
With one amazingly wonderous feature
It has a proboscis that's long and slim
and can do anything with it, on a whim.
They can lift, graze, drink or snap
Be gentle or give a mighty slap
But the thing that's best, without fail
Is when they use it to hold mum's tail.

Mike Hamill

Hedge The Hedgehog

There's been a little visitor, not sure if he or she
but they've been in my garden and left a gift for me!
I know not where they've been, throughout the long dark night,
but now they will be sleeping, in the day's brightest light.

I have had a little visitor; they've not been here for a while.
So even their little deposit, brought forth a warming smile.
Hopefully, I will hear it, snuffling in the evening's chill,
and no matter if boy or girl, the sound will be a thrill!

I have had a little visitor; I'm calling them Hedge?
I'll enjoy their company; this is my honest pledge!
I'm sure now that Hedge is male. Now this is not a slur!
But, if Hedge was a female, she'd clean up after her!

The Buffoon

I spoke words wisdom to the buffoon,
whose attention wandered; far too soon.
The idiot smiled his crooked grin,
His breath tinged lightly, with the scent of gin.

His clothes were nautical. Of sorts.
Hawaiian shirt and Bermuda shorts.
Toenails painted Red, Blue and Green
Such a sight you've never seen.

The time came to bid him farewell,
and, on his departure I did dwell.
And, with some reflection, did I ponder.
As I passed the mirror, I did wonder?

Mike Hamill

Georgie

There was a giraffe called Georgie,
Who was tall and oh so haughty.
But felt quite a chump,
When given a thump
By his dad for being so naughty

The Question Resolved

The ayes have it the owl said
as, with gravitas he bowed his head.
"Hear, hear," cried the gathered throng,
and the larks all burst into song
The parliament of owls had convened
To answer a question of academe
And all the creatures that walked or flew
And those that crawled were all there too
To listen to the owl, speak with conviction and might
And declare there's nothing wrong with toast and marmite!

Mike Hamill

The Purple Crane

I came across a purple crane,
next to him, I felt quite plain.
He squawked a bit and made a noise
He stood upright, such an arrogant poise.
He stretched his wings, oh so wide,
and gently, each feather he modified.
The feathers had a translucent sheen
Shades of pink and aquamarine
He was a handsome fellow. That's the truth,
and he stared at me with gimlet eyes of puce.
His beak was open, I could see right in
And it was filled, right to the brim.
For there, inside that cavernous mouth,
were three frogs and a river trout.
He said to me in a dulcet voice,
"Welcome to tea, please make your choice."
I bade him thanks, but politely declined.
So, on his own he now dined.

Pretty Boy

He strode the street, looking cute,
in his brand new, yellow polka dotted suit.
In the windows, as he passed by,
his perfect reflection caught his eye.
He was the perennial popinjay,
who paraded the town every day.
Pretty boy, was his pseudonym,
and his hair was brushed, all neat and trim.
All his admirers he did beguile,
and bestowed on them a benevolent smile.
He was the coolest cat. Laid back and mellow,
in his suit of polka dots in yellow.
The foxy ladies thought he was great,
the guys just wanted to be his mate.
But now his promenade is all done,
and he's off for tea with his dad and mum.

Mike Hamill

The Dragonfly

From fast running streams or stagnant ponds
rises a creature that climbs the watery fronds.
They complete the osmosis from the deep,
as they gently wait and quietly sleep.
And then, they break free from the aquatic chain
and emerge translucent, beautiful. No longer plain!
They climb their perch, spread wings and fly,
and for a short time; they are The Dragonfly!

A Purple Road

Upon a purple pathway,
I dreamt of yesterday.
Of coloured flying creatures
that came with me to play.

Six legged elephants,
with purple pointed trunks.
With green embroidered accoutrements,
and three polka dotted skunks.

Above me is a primrose sky,
with fluffy clouds of pink.
And floating past my jaundiced eye
the biggest kitchen sink.

Upon the plains of Xanadu
A spotted zebra did I spy
She wore a yellow tutu
And an orange painted tie

We danced the hokey cokey,
and finished with a Twist.
We sang some karaoke!
The meerkats did assist.

Mike Hamill

The party kept on going,
until the midnight broke.
And soon the sun was glowing,
as from my dream I woke.

Octopussy

Yesterday, I passed an octopus on the street.
He smiled and raised his cap. It was so sweet.
He ambled along and occasionally stopped,
for this was the day that he usually shopped.
He did purchase mussels, crab and shrimps by the score,
All of which he did adore.
He'd glide over the street on his tentacles,
all covered in seaweed and barnacles.
He smiled at children and petted a dog,
and, once, he even kissed a hedgehog.
But, only once, as it was a mistake,
he'd thought the hedgehog was a cake
And now, back to the ocean he swiftly trots
until, up ahead, a friend he spots.
"Hello squiddy" he said. "You're so nice to see.
Come to my house, we can partake of tea.
Mussel cake, with Raspberry soup,
served delicately in a glass coupe.
Crab, served with fromage bombardier.
All washed down with a shrimp beer."
"Why Octi, that's very spiffing, I must say.
You have just made my perfect day."

Mike Hamill

So, with tentacles linked, they sashayed away.
Into the ocean, through the waves fine spray.
To feast and chatter till it was time for supper.
But all that was left, was bread and cockle butter.

Quentin The Caterpillar

Quentin the caterpillar quickly walked
while beside him, Horace talked and talked.
They spoke of things they would do today.
Of what they'd eat. Of games they'd play.
And oh, the cabbage leaves they'd munch
as they ate a pleasant, leisurely lunch.

As they wandered through the cabbage patch
on occasion, Quentin would snatch,
a minute or two of quiet reflection.
As he considered, sadly, his complexion.
He'd think and hope and heave a sigh
And wished one day of being a butterfly.

Mike Hamill

The Storm

It comes, rolling in from the West,
and meets the East, breast to breast.
The deep dark waves crash down with vigour
and beat the coast with utmost anger.

The foam tipped waves crash on shingle
Where unknown footsteps intermingle
Upon the skies, the lightning flashes
As the thunder screams and loudly crashes.

The Eastern shore takes the flood,
it drives the watchers from where they stood.
On hilly dunes of salt crushed grass,
to not return. Alas, alas.

Beyond the beach, the waves, the sea,
I feel the storm calling me.
It whispers loudly. It screams at me
And then, it's gone. Finally.

The Coral Steps

See the tiny coral steps
That lead down. Down to the depths
Through the subterranean passage do they go
To whom knows what? Far below.

Slick and shiny the steps become,
as they are hidden from the sun.
And, in the hidden passage, as we go,
fluorescent creatures bathe us in their glow.

And at last, the steps do cease,
And into the sea we are released.
To walk with the magical creatures here
In waters, both calm and clear.

See the sea nymphs as they play,
racing on seahorses; on kelp strewn brae.
The sea dragons dance on rolling waves
As they chase and whoop like warrior braves.

See Poseidon with his cohort ride.
His guard of merman by his side.
His chariot pulled by six white sharks
the King of all aquatic monarchs.

Mike Hamill

All to soon it is time to return.
And to the surface we must adjourn.
Once again to climb those coral steps,
and, on our adventures to reflect.

Oh, the secrets that we have seen
and met with Amphitrite. Poseidon's' Queen.
And to dream of the next time our footsteps
will lead us to mysteries. Down the coral steps.

Jack in London

The swirling mist, through cobbled streets does flow,
where gas lamps bequeath a dim and dreary glow.
The dampness of the mist combines with fabled London smog
And so, begins each night, London's prologue.
The gents all strut in evening wear. Top hats and tails
The ladies gather in drawing rooms where such gossip does prevail.
The streets are dim, the alehouses, loud, raucous and brash.
Where footpads and the cutpurse lurk, to relieve folk of their cash.
The ladies of the night parade, their gifts on open show
And, in the darkest corners there, philanderers will go.
A street girl smiles and offers up her wares
The offer accepted; another customer she snares.
But down some dirt filled alleyway, where rats and cockroach play,
the girl now lies silently. Her lifeblood slips away.
A scream is heard. A peeler runs, whistle to his lips
And through London's fog filled night, Jack the ripper slips.

Mike Hamill

Morning

The clouds do part, the covers rise,
the veil of darkness clears my eyes.
The dawn breaks, the daylight starts
As Selene slowly now departs
Hypnos leaves me for the sun
And will return when darkness come.

The Day

The cock crowed, it's half past three.
Dawn has broken, time for tea.
Then he crowed just for those,
still asleep, in repose.

In the air the Swifts and Swallows fly,
calling gently in the morning sky.
Dancing, pirouetting on a par,
with every human, ballet star.

In the ponds and riverbeds,
fish and crustaceans raise their heads.
To bask in each warming ray,
in salutation to a summer's day.

Then, the badgers sniff the morning air.
Time for bed, they do declare.
To their sets they now creep,
to spend their day. Fast asleep.

Mike Hamill

Nighttime Dreams

Another night of endless dreams
of dragon fights and evil queens.
Of riding out on a fiery path,
to battle for justice. At last.

A night of screeching calling owls.
Familiars all from earth's dark bowels.
Who flap and flutter at my skin,
as the darkness stumbles in

But then I see the faintest light,
as daytime drives away the night.
The church clock chimes. New day begins.
And washes away nighttime sins.

And now into that light I meander,
no more to nighttime demons' pander.
The daytime sun looks down to say,
welcome, to another day.

Mountainsides

The sun rises,
in hazy guises.
But winters hold,
brings the cold.

Winds blow,
to valleys below.
Ice gleams,
on streets and streams.

Fast rides,
down mountainsides.
Softest snow,
as swift we go.

Grey skies,
the Eagle cries.
Drifting past,
on thermal draughts.

On mountains sheer,
with no fear.
Walk Mountain goats,
in furry coats.

Mike Hamill

My heartbeat rises,
the view hypnotizes.
A new day's birth,
on God's great earth.

The Autumn

The Autumn colours creep through the trees,
Reds. Golds and Browns make a multi coloured frieze.
Amidst the reed beds ominous and dark
The corncrake readies to depart,
The elusive Bittern lifts his eyes,
As summer visitors reach for the skies.

Amidst the gardens and forests fall,
The creatures ready for the winters call.
Squirrels scurry to fill their larder full.
While others work to their own schedule.
All to wait for winters awful bite
But protected, warm, and out of sight

To the skies above, my eyes are drawn.
Autumn sunshine, colours of ripened corn.
Clouds that billow and fight together
And bring fresh rain. Autumnal weather!
They tumble in laughter across the skies
Winters coming you can hear in their whispered sighs

Mike Hamill

But its Autumn that gives us such glorious hope
As she and summer finally do elope!
And soon their only child will joyfully sing
And that child? Its name is Spring
Then such joy on all will befall
As Spring, winters grip; does overhaul.

My Garden & Other Poems

The Journey

I wandered through a churchyard fair
and the many people standing there.
Striking conversations we did employ.
Oh, the reminiscing. Oh, such joy.

The evening light in dapple shades,
strikes the mounds of grassy blades.
In the road, beyond the lychgate,
the gentries' carriages quietly wait.

The clock tower tolls the twilight hour.
The birds fly startled, from the bower.
They flutter in the setting sun,
as the evening has now begun.

And now as the darkness finally falls,
I take my steps to the drinking halls.
And there, with ale and friendship to imbibe.
And then, on my horse, will homeward ride.

Mike Hamill

Perfect Lines

The perfect lines,
of shuttered blinds,
bring calmness close behind.

The dust motes dance,
mesmerise, entrance,
in bewildering circumstance.

The suns hot rays,
in diamond displays,
will brook no suspects malaise.

The chase is on,
who will begone,
once across the Rubicon?

I fear no deed,
I will proceed,
no avenue will I cede.

Come mornings day,
the nighttime sway,
again, is held at bay!

The dream has flown,
my stature grown,
the future golden. But unknown.

Mike Hamill

Shapes

Dark, shifting shapes. People I never knew!
Passing by; just strangers. Oh, so many, oh so few.
Whispered voices. Are they calling me?
Should I answer them? Will it set them free?

Dark passing shapes, drifting in the gloom.
Will I see their faces in the silver moon?
Gathered in milling throngs of shining bright,
oh, they chatter through the fiery light.

Dark shifting shapes metamorph to grey,
in the light of the coming day.
The indistinct shapes begin to form,
as strangers become friends in the mornings dawn

Goodnight Mama

Good night mama I gently weep,
close your eyes now. Go to sleep.
I touch the face that smiled at me,
picked me up and made me, me!
That kissed the cuts and running tears
and drove away my frightened fears,
who turned my nighttime into day.
I love you Mama is all I can say.

Mike Hamill

Another Springtime Day

Winds rattle against panes of glass.
Hailstones melt, on fresh green grass.
Rainstorms pass in shades of grey,
    just another springtime day.

Clouds darken the skies of blue,
    showing black in every hue.
Umbrellas block the people's way.
    Just another springtime day.

Waves roil in spume and foam.
The visions. All in monochrome.
The Gods have issued a communique,
    just another springtime day.

Thunder comes, lightning too.
Crashing, flashing. The storms renew.
The wildness, the power, natures display.
    Just another, springtime day.

The clouds now part, the sun breaks out,
    we lift our eyes and loudly shout!
As soft breezes now through trees do play.
    It's just another springtime day.

Consternation

I am in consternation.
My brains in dehydration,
I have cranial constipation.
Such a complication.

I must, once more dig deep.
And forfeit my nightly sleep
A chasm I must leap
Else, with tears I might weep

The words have temporarily ceased.
My personal dictionary's deceased,
No words can be released!
My inspirations decreased.

Mike Hamill

Can You See?

Can you see the skies at night
touch the stars shining bright,
hear the silence twixt the sound.
Does the Earth go round and round?

Do the rivers flow to the sea
can the air be truly free?
Does the moon wax and wane?
Can the earth feel the same?

Do the words that we exhale
on others minds forcibly impale.
Can we, on our laurels rest
are our lives just a test?

I see the star's most every night
in the heavens shining bright.
I hear the silences voices bring.
It lifts my heart, and I will sing

Dawn Breaks

Dawn breaks, the sun rises,
the day comes with surprises.
Feet clatter,
folk chatter,
and opportunity entices.

Evening comes, the moon ascends,
and spectres soon impend.
Ghostly walks,
whispered talks,
then sleep does attend.

Mike Hamill

Destitution

Dreamy spires of ancient towns,
wreathed in mystique did abound.
In cobbled streets where hackneys ran,
drays refuel the ale-house man.

The church bells all, ringing out
calling the gentry, all faithful and devout,
into prayer and contemplation.
The choir boys drifting to temptation!

Smoke from blackened fires flow,
and in the hearths, the embers grow.
Women old before their time,
chatter ceaselessly on a factory line.

Men with twisted limbs and worn-out backs
walk the streets in feral packs.
Seeking help and restitution,
to escape the poorhouse institution.

To their houses, the gentry will parade
Where waits the servant and the maid.
But tell me. What do the poor acquire
Amidst each lofty, dreaming, spire?

Dreams

Dreams are memories now long past,
of pleasant interludes or deeds surpassed.
Of living life, of friends you know.
Of fighting dragons, blow by blow.
Of tasty meals, the sweetest things.
Of listening as the choir sings.
Of pleasures great and pleasures small.
that into your life does call.

Mike Hamill

Evening Scenes

Each ray of light in soft diffusion
spreads mystical and surreal confusion.
As creeping tendrils fall to the ground,
ethereal shadows dance around.

The misty cloak envelopes all
and holds us in a spectral thrall.
It takes the day in a silent hold
and brings forth such mysteries untold!

Of dancing lights in a zephyr wind,
of ghostly shapes that whirl and swim.
Of quiet voices that unseen,
incorporeal gatherings do convene.

They follow behind the cicerone,
who leads them to the eyried throne,
where nymphs and faeries do display
until the daylight takes them away.

My Garden & Other Poems

Endless nights

Endless nights
when dim streetlights
on wet streets gently glow.

The night shift heads
towards their bed.
Their weariness does grow.

A car now starts,
the day shift departs.
Can you hear the Cockerel crow?

The milk floats clatter,
the delivery folk chatter,
the day begins to grow.

Out of the dark,
the brightening spark,
is the new day all aglow!

The day is filled.
As hours are spilled.
And the world puts on a show.

Mike Hamill

Again, the darkness falls
and a night bird calls.
The pace begins to slow.

The house lights bright
and the car's headlight,
ghostly tableaux do bestow.

And on damp streets,
the night shifts creep,
and footsteps slowly go.

Lost Memories

Back in the day, so many years ago.
Things were different don't you know.
No electronic games or mobile phones,
no Instagram, WhatsApp or flying drones.
Kids running about, having a great time.
When I was a kid back in '59.
Scuffed shoes and knees all skinned.
Hair parted and neatly trimmed.
Cowboys and Indians; guns and stuff,
And playtimes were sometimes, a little rough!
Out playing until it was dark,
Going scrumping; such a lark.
You knew the Bobby on the beat,
He'd dispense both thick ear, or treat!
I miss those days as I grow old,
But they weren't PC! Or so I'm told!
But who cares? It was just a magic time
When I was 10. In '59

Mike Hamill

Good Night

Good night sweet lady,
lay your head down and think of me.
We walk the water's edge hand in hand,
the water shimmers in the grey moonlight bloom,
and fluoresces as we, like children play.
We run, laugh and tumble in the dark wet sand
And think of places. Over there. A way away!
We hold each other, when we stand; together.
Good night sweet lady
Lay your head down now sleep.
And think of me.

Hands Touch

Hands touch at the occasion,
fingers entwined for the duration.
Hearts beats in adoration,
words flow in exultation.
Lips touch in sweet persuasion,
tongues caress in mutual invasion.
Minds meet in expectation!

Mike Hamill

Mother, Maiden & Crone

I look to the firmament, celestial winds are blown
And there live the Maiden, Mother and Crone
Selene of the Greeks shines a benevolent smile
As across the heavens begins the nightly trial

The Roman Luna rides the skies this night
And crosses before us, perfect and bright
This silver disk, this glistening stone
Home of the Maiden, Mother and Crone

Stirring deeds, will I tell, if I could
With silver ink, the moons lifeblood
Stories of beauty and love that are true
But I must not. So, the moon I stole for you.

Light over Dark

I stood alone 'twixt unknown faces,
in darkened rooms and unknown places.
I hear a cacophony of unknown noise.
I hear no laughter, sense no joys.
I look around this unfriending place,
no hope, no warmth, no loving space.
I hear no movement; I sense no sound
as all about me, move around.
But I wait. For on a distant, distant hill,
I hear laughter! It touches me with a thrill.
The lightness grows, the dark shadows fade,
I see the colours before me arrayed!

I see the light, it dazzles me
with its very intensity
I feel a kindred spirit close by,
as we come together by and by.
A gentle touch some sage advice
I drop the blinkers from my eyes
Before me stands, hopefully a friend.
And now it has started please, let it not end
as we travel on a journey of laughter, colours and light
or sit beneath a starry, evening night.
And talk of things gone and past.
Memories cherished but stored at last!

Mike Hamill

My Eyes Are Closed

My eyes are closed I see the world.
My ears are shut, the dreams unfurl.
My mouth is closed, no words are spoken,
the memories are all here; unbroken.

I take a step, but nothing changed.
The words are there, prearranged.
I hear no voices, but they all speak,
with one tongue they do critique.

I feel the warmth, where is the sun?
Upon my face, the heat's begun.
I sense the smiles that do abound.
it's good to see my friends around.

My New Sisters

I have my new sisters now, to share my memories with.
To chatter and renew, the times that we have lived.
To hold close, right by my side, inside my heart.
To have found them at last. No more times apart!
I have to say my sisters, and what I say it true.
I'm glad I've found my sisters; and that those sisters are you.

Mike Hamill

Old Age Is No Fun

The midnight hour has just struck.
And once again I'm out of luck.
So, to the bathroom, I must go,
this just ain't fun, don't you know.

It's one o'clock, I'm off again,
I'm sure I'll end up quite insane.
My night is made of little trips,
It really, really is the pits!

The time is now half past two
I'm off again, to the loo.
The journey now is quite familiar.
The purpose? Oh, so very similar.

The clock is showing just after three.
And I'm gone again, for another wee!
When, from this burden will I be free?
This is not a time of Christmas Glee.

The church bell chimes it's now gone four.
I cannot, really, do much more.
I close my eyes. Will I sleep?
Oh no! My bladders got a date to keep!

The tale repeats every hour.
At six I'm up, for my shower.
I'll have a change of scenery too.
And go and use the downstairs loo!

Mike Hamill

The Kiss

What is a kiss, but a light glancing touch.
But oh, it can mean so, so much.
The meeting of two pairs of lips,
where joy and sorrow can eclipse.

A soft gentle brush in passing,
A soulful joining, everlasting.
A kiss that says you are my friend
and this, all else does transcend!

The confounding of our thought,
as each new joy is brought.
The excitement as our lips do part
and exploring tongues swiftly dart.

Each new pleasure brings a degree,
of fresh joy and are passions free?
The pleasure I hope we both perceive,
as each kiss we do retrieve

Nature

See the mist, eerie shadows make.
As it drifts, forlornly, cross meadow and lake.
I smell the dampness all around,
as its fingers descend to the ground.

I hear the whistling in the trees,
and feel the gentle, whispering breeze.
The forest trees all gently sway,
as on the forest floor, the creatures play.

I hear the song the early birds do sing,
the silent owl out on the wing.
I hear the fox cubs by the den at play,
as mother seeks the waiting prey!

To the riverbanks, so green and lush
the waterfowl, so swiftly rush.
The vulpine bark on the night wind sings,
and they seek the safety the water brings.

Not all escape the hunter's claw,
sharpened teeth or gaping maw!
A squeal, a flurry of panicked feet!
Too late, too late; the owl will eat!

Mike Hamill

Requiem For Nigel

He came to us a man of some stature.
Hirsute, smiling, like a parochial pastor.
With an essence of garlic and mind-blowing farts
Nigel was a man of many, many parts!
From Monk, Leper or when suited with helm
A champion, a true knight of the realm?
He brings his humour that he willingly imparts
And, have I mentioned, the garlic and farts?
Sleep well Nigel, as now you have gone.
A man who was, to all who knew him, just fun.
Irreplaceable, unique just one of a kind
who in life, became a friend of mine.
Now, he is up there, with St. Peter and friends,
to regale with stories, blasphemous to the end.
But God will be happy, with this lionheart
and take him all. Yes, including each garlic fart!
RIP Nigel

Cake

Oft times I ponder as night closes in,
whether indulgence is really a sin?
Can I perchance; and I whisper just to you
have my cake and eat it too?

Can I, the Devil's advocate be and plot?
And covet those things that I should not?
Can I choose unwisely, bad decisions make.
And eat forever, more chocolate and cake?

Can I ignore, as the corpulence grows,
the finding of forever, shrinking clothes?
Can I make promises to really stay trim?
And forget them totally; when there's cake in the tin?

Mike Hamill

Shadows

Can you see the shadows, dancing in the gloom,
Iridescent moonbeams by the night consumed?
Hiding in the darkness, their intent unknown,
can you approach them, before they have flown?
Silvered filigree confusions, upon the streets they prance.
They tiptoe so softly, and now they advance.
Then vanish so quickly, beneath each tall streetlamp,
that shines in muted yellows in the cold and misty damp.
I see those fleeting ghosts, that swirl around each street
and I run in confusion, not wishing to meet.
They gather in profusion, a writhing phantom swarm.
Then disappear quickly as comes the morning's dawn.

Pain

The darkness comes, the pain returns and envelopes me.

The shining light that was your face, is no longer there too see?

I miss the caress of your sweet words, they calmed my hidden fears,

and now they are no longer there, just washed away in tears!

Friends we've been and so we will remain.

And, when we talk and laugh and joke; I'll hide from you my pain

Mike Hamill

Solitude

The room is crowded, but no-one is there!
The noise is loud; but I cannot hear!
The views are breath-taking; but nothing I see,
the gift is life; but not for free!

I pace the room; but I cannot move.
I smell the flowers; but I cannot choose.
I touch your face; but I cannot feel.
I take a breath; but nothing's real.

I watch the sunrise; but just feel the cold.
see the moonrise; but just feel old.
see the stars; but nothing glitters in the sky!
feel the tears, but I cannot cry.

Starlings

They come crashing in, a uniformed horde
filling trees, bushes and greensward.
They chatter back and forth and create
a single entity, who's noise does permeate,
the very ears and brains of all who hear.
Their attitude? So aggressive and cavalier.
Calling out to those who would think to invade
With harsh messages conveyed.
And then, when the feast is complete
or the leading majority are replete,
they lift, amidst the whirring rush
of feathered wings that them, upward push.
And in the sky a ballet they perform
with shapes and sounds that don't conform,
to things we understand.
And is still, beyond the wit of man.
And gradually, as the evening light does fade,
another murmuration is unmade.
And then, as the dying sun gives its final boost,
the silence slowly comes, as the birds all roost

Mike Hamill

The Stars

I saw the stars like chandeliers,
a million glistening diamond tears.
They shone, this jewelled enormity.
The epitome of antiquity.

And then, in perfect harmony,
the planets did align for me
In astronomical equality
And celestial equanimity!

I saw the moon turn its face,
as across empyrean skies it does race.
Fleeing once again before the sun,
Until the day, again, becomes undone.

Then the evening stars again shine bright,
showing travellers, the guiding light.
To bring them safely from journeys made,
till softly on the pillow, their head is laid!

And then as Hypnos guides our sleep
and Nyx does the night skies keep.
We rest until there comes the morn
when Eos brings once more the dawn!

Summertime

I love the Sunshine, each bright new dawn.
The scent of summer that permeates each morn.
Walks by bubbling riverbanks or sandy seashore.
Walking hand in hand, through the forest's carpeted floor.
I love the gentle fall of summer rain,
that barely leaves behind its wet stain
on hot fields, or well-trod street.
The upturned faces of strangers that we meet.
Smiling, welcoming as we stroll by.
A gentle nod, a tip of the hat and a smiling hi.
I love the sound of children playing in the park
the songbirds singing, thrush and soaring lark.
There, the gossamer winged dragonfly
flitting swiftly, chasing mates that they espy
I love to watch the moonrise on a cloudless night
till the sun rises again; warming and bright.

Mike Hamill

Tenements

On grass-filled streets, by cracked pavements bound.
The life and sound,
of Tenement folk in each smoke-filled home.
where families live and vermin roam.
And adults trudge in rain and shine,
to cotton mill or gas-filled mine.
To labour hard at the owner's will
and escape the poorhouse treadmill.
The children play with sticks and stones,
all dirty faces, all skin and bones.
But soon their childhood will be no more,
as they scurry neath the ravenous maw
of rattling looms, that sing, and spin
and drag unwary children in.

My Garden & Other Poems

The Birds

I see them up, oh so high,
performing ballet in the sky.
Feathered creatures big and small.
All performing at the avian ball.

Kite's, Buzzard's, Osprey too,
the downy Owl's soft twit twoo!
The Starlings amazing murmuration,
the pigeons causing devastation!

The Blue tits with their cheeky call.
The feisty Sparrows shout and brawl.
The Kingfisher in his translucent plumes,
arrow straight into the river zooms.

The flying visitors from lands afar,
the beautiful song of each nightjar.
These and many more lift our lives,
let's protect them and ensure, each one survives.

Mike Hamill

The Fading Sun

The fading sun caresses each rising peak
and winter solstice brings forth, pagan mystique.
The ancients gather in druidic throngs
and call the Gods in foreign tongues.

The sunbeams play on valley floors
and repeat their dance in fierce encores.
The beasts roam midst the valley green
as in herds of magnitude they do convene.

The light dances a pas-de-deux,
and with the wind does debut.
They glide across this waking land
dancing together, hand in hand.

The winter sun fades into disarray,
as into the trees the duo stray.
In dank forests, the rays now falter
as the darkness, they do encounter!

The weak luminescence's strengthen
as the days grow and slowly lengthen.
The druid's prayers have been fulfilled.
As winters grip is once more distilled.

My Garden & Other Poems

The Garden

The first blooms rise and shake their heads,
and converse in Snowdrop around the beds.
The other flowers soon follow suit,
and the conversation as always, is somewhat moot

They dream of phosphate vitamin-rich
Or Sequestered iron, the perfect switch
They talk of sunshine, rain, and feed
And they look down upon the little weed.

There are snails, insects, the occasional slug
all superfood to the passing frog.
His tongue extends, he begins to grin
as each tasty morsel pops right in!

The garden looks great, including the Gnome,
as the birds all look, for a brand-new home
to raise a brood of fluffy chick's
In houses of wood, stones and sticks.

It's the greatest time to enjoy the scene,
of colourful flowers and grass so green.
Of fledging birds. Once cute little chick's
now abandoning those homes of stones and sticks.

Mike Hamill

I Touch

I touch, I stroke and gently sip
As into the wetness I do slip!
I taste the sweetness, oh so fine.
I need much more, is that a crime?
My hands enfold a pert, round shape
as, for a moment, to ecstasy I escape!
Oh, such is the exquisite bliss
At the mornings first, lovely kiss.
As my lips meet hers, I feel the heat
upon my tongue as we do greet.
I feel the warmth that envelopes me
As I drink my morning, first coffee!

The Moon

The land shimmers in a ghostly iridescence
as moonbeams and shadows gently dance.
Shapes shift as creatures dart from light to dark.
Wary of the silent beat of falling wings or fox's bark!

Diana, the huntress, walks the shadowed hills
as her sister, the moon, the nighttime fills.
With her spectral glow, shining so bright,
it turns the Stygian darkness into light!

The waters in the babbling brooks and woodland lakes
shine in opalescent grandeur, as moonlight breaks.
And, above, bathed in her gentle light, sleep roosting birds
a close packed symmetry of gathered avian herds.

And still the moon, that luminous shimmering disc,
fills the empyrean sky and marches, at a pace so brisk.
Across the firmament in perpetual ethereal motion,
to clear the heavens for the dawning solar convocation.

And now, harried by the sun God she does depart!
This is not the end, but the beginning of a new start.
For soon her gentle light will once more glow
and give moonlights soft spectral luminescence. To all below.

Mike Hamill

The Dance

The music plays. Do you hear the beat?
Does it make you want to move your feet?
In steps and rhythms that are involuntary
But now, age restrictions; keep it precautionary!

In your youth, did you boogie about
Or perhaps, just Twist and Shout?
Did you Jive or do the Lindy hop?
Groove to the music, or just bop?

Can you cut a rug or do the Palais glide?
Waltz or quickstep, that's so dignified.
No matter your dance, be enthusiastic
as you trip away with the light fantastic.

The River

I sit beside a babbling brook and listen to its song.
I see the minnows gather, in a darting lively throng.
In shallow pools that dribble over algae covered rock,
I watch the river's passage. To the sea it does drop.
I see a flash of blue and green that darts from the trees beside.
And the male kingfisher rises, with a gift for his waiting bride.
And now, the river widens and slows its rushing pace,
And, from its turbulent start, is now filled with lazy grace.
The waters clear and beneath the dribbling flow,
Larvae, and aquatic life, in its weed filled shallows grow.
The wildfowl hide amongst the wilderness of blooming Rush and Sedge,
And patient fishermen sit quietly, by the rivers soft banked edge.
With practised wrists, they cast their hand tied flies, in gentle, poetic flight
And wait for trout and salmon to rise to a final hungry bite.
And now the journeys end, and the water makes the final leap.
As it bids farewell to the land and joins the ocean deep.

Mike Hamill

The Stream

The river flows downstream apace,
the meadow and the pastures graced.
The burbling brook slips from its source
and runs along its natural course.
Its tumbling waters gather stone
and to aquatic life is home.
The hunted in the turbulence glide
amidst the detritus, from the hunters, they hide.
But none are safe from the skies
when by the kingfisher they are spied!
A glimpse of blue, a translucent flash.
And avian death comes in a splash.
But onward runs the river, free,
heading ever to the sea.
With no thought of things, it has past
just the coast; and to be free at last.

The Train

It glides through the hills and plains
in rhythmic sound that slowly wanes.
As swirling clouds of billowing smoke
drift slowly overland. To cloak
the countryside in a warming mist
which the mighty beast has one-time kissed.
And, in its burning belly, the coals do glow
and to the night sky, fire imps it does throw.
Which create a fiery dancing sprite
that lightens up the winter's night.
Now, the Flying Scotsman does strip
the miles; and makes its final trip!
Up to the North and Scotland's pride
To Edinburgh, it makes its final ride.

Mike Hamill

The Wind

The summer breezes like a zephyr float, amongst the dappled trees,
it twists and turns like a fluid snake and bends the waiting leaves.
And, as it escapes the forest's dark confine,
the powers of the earth and air it will combine
and the zephyr is no more a gentle wind
cavorting and undisciplined.

It has changed. Metamorphosed to a stiff, strong breeze,
that clatters all in its path and ruffles the seas.
It dashes over the waiting broads, and heads to freedom beyond.
It dances across still waters as, with impunity, it does abscond.

Can you hear the water birds sing their collective song?
as they cluster at the Broads soft edge, a gaggling calling throng?
The bittern and corncrake boom, from deep within the rush and sedge.
The ducks and coots paddle swiftly, from the banks soft sloping edge.
They seek from within the murky depths, the detritus and weed
the larvae and other things on which they greedily feed.

In the marina, the passing wind trails soft white petticoats
and sends a quiver through the halyards of the waiting sailing boats.
As the sails at the main mast gently begin to slap,
the sailors raise a smile, and children start to clap.
Raise the mainsheet, a small wee voice does cry,
and smiling adults' rush; to eagerly comply.

Soon the water is filled, with boats that move to and fro,
as round and round in joyous chase they swiftly do go.
The crack of canvas as they tack, the creaking of the tiller,
the raucous shouts to the crew of each excited skipper.
But the wind cares not and onwards it does go
passing over sailing boats and coasts; to where? I'll never know!

Mike Hamill

Twilight

The sun begins its decline and falls to the west.
The sky darkens at its overpowering behest.
And, just as the Sun approaches its nadir,
the twilight shadows stretch from there to here.
The shadows lengthen and nightfall comes
and to the night our world succumbs.
And, as the light gently fades away,
twilight is the change twixt night and day.
In its shadows, the nighttime creatures' shuffle.
Slipping silently onward with the barest rustle.
Now, as the evening light does fail and falter,
twilight departs, on the cusp of Selene's heavenly Altar!
She will return at a time opportune,
but now she sleeps, twixt sun and moon.
Soon, twilight's gossamer light will persevere
And the evening shadows will stretch again, from there to here

The Starlight

The starlight dims as you appear,
the heavens firmament seems austere.
I feel your breath upon my face,
your heavenly scent I can't erase.
It swims around inside my mind
where, forever, it is consigned.
A memory to recall when you're not here.
to calm me when the nights' dark draws near
I watch the moon in celestial navigation
And know she shines on you, in admiration.

Mike Hamill

Spring

Empty avenues and untrodden streets,
a snowy capped mountain's soaring peaks.
The eagle's eyrie alone, forlorn,
the harvest mouse amongst the corn.
The sun's weak rays that gather strength,
and daylight hours that increase in length.

New buds that break the earth and stand
in an increasing, multi-coloured, floral band.
As mother nature breaks winters tight hold
and springtime's cornucopia does unfold.

And the creatures of the sea, land, and air
do bring forth new life, in joyous fanfare.
As once more comes wonderous spring,
a cacophony of sound and colour does it bring.

Amongst those silent avenues and quiet streets,
wherein the soul of man quietly beats,
there comes a belief and a rising desire
that winters hard breath will soon expire.

Valhalla

I look above the silent trees,
that sway so gently in the breeze.
And watch the shadows creep and slide,
and see the Valkyries ghostly ride.
They choose from those who must fall
To sit in Askard, Odin's Hall!
They hear the tales and songs of those
Who fell before and then arose
A seat in Valhalla welcomes all,
who stand with Odin at the call
to Ragnarök. And then again to fall.

Mike Hamill

A Winter Morning

The winter light shines dim and grey
as morning darkness slips away.
Jack Frost has been and passed on by
his frozen breath a whispered sigh.
It's left his mark on boughs and trees.
in patterned, covered frosty sleeves!

The morning birds in plump feathered coats,
call the days start from within their throats.
And all around in houses dark, the people rise
and wipe the night dust from their eyes.
And soon the sun will dimly light
the day, until again winter, early brings the night!

It's 2 AM

It's 2 am the moonlight glows,
as through my window it's luminescence flows.
Selene once more patrols the sky,
as Hypnos denies me sleep. Oh why?

It's 3 am, the night stars glitter,
I see them as I lie here!
They are such an arresting sight
In the dark firmament of the night!

It's 4 am, from my window no lights I see,
just a strange apparition looks back at me.
I see myself, my weary eyes
that tire of gazing at the skies!

It's 5 am, I see the dawn,
as gradually, comes the morn.
My head, upon my pillow rests.
But sleep still is not to be my guest!

It's 6 am the people rise,
and go about their daily lives.
But I still desire a somnolent state.
But, in vain I do wait.

Mike Hamill

It's 7 am and Nyx has gone.
As has Hypnos, her wandering son.
I hope they return, and a promise keep,
to give me rest. To give me sleep!

The Nighttime

The corners of my mind appear.
And therein grows the tree of fear.
No brightness lights each new day start.
No hues of sunshine do impart
the monochromatic hues of black and grey
that starts the dawning of each day.

My eyes look inward to find my soul,
a broken, dishevelled, leaking bowl.
Where pours forth the froth of spirit
that gathers in the depths within it
and boils away to warm the cold
that leaches, slowly as I grow old.

What comes to me from there.
that place? I know not where!
And doors are slammed, and keys are turned
where the joy of life is spurned:
and sleep is denied forever I cry!
And I am extinguished, with a sigh!

Mike Hamill

Will-o'-the-Wisp

I saw a wonderous thing last night
gilded in the silvery moonlight.
A creature so fine, yet so frail.
A cap of yellow and a glowing tail.
With eyes that sparked like St Elmos fire,
and an energy that did never tire.
It danced like a will-o'-the-wisp
and its smile did persist,
in laughter and exuberance
as through my mind it did prance.
It filled my head with warmth and bliss
And softly, my heart it kissed.
So now I send this creature just to you.
So that you, these pleasures, can accrue

Dappled Glades

Underneath, where the great oak sits
and the willow, into the passing water dips.
In sleepy hollows and shaded glades,
were children have, in laughter played.
There I see the flowers bloom,
and scent the forest in sweet perfume.
The musical trill of birds in flight.
The dappled shades assault the sight
in tinctures of multicoloured hues.
The senses, they do overwhelm and confuse.
The forest, this home of nature's best,
where happily, I will sit and rest.

Mike Hamill

On The Beach

Each footstep in wet sand does shimmer.
And, on the bandstand instruments glimmer.
Crowds gather around in an expectant throng.
Ready and waiting to burst into song.
Picnics are waiting, to be eaten at leisure,
father sips ale and murmurs with pleasure.
Kids roam beaches, parent free,
wondering, what mums brought for tea?
Excitedly gathered in raucous congregation,
waiting for drama in tense anticipation.
Punch and Judy, the eternal battle does fight,
as small faces beam and scream in delight.
Grandmother sits with stockings rolled down
hat akimbo and wearing a frown.
Grandad, in his Sunday suit does sit.
His paper unread. His pipe unlit.
Donkeys trotting, up and down,
oh, those summers, in an English Seaside town.

Whispers

You listen to me in a whisper,
our voices barely heard.
Within the mighty amphitheatre,
our voices are interred.

We cry a tear that slowly,
down our cheek does run.
And plunges ever lowly,
beneath the summers sun.

These tears bring us memories,
that enliven the night.
Stored forever in treasuries,
that glimmer in the light.

That brings us life and sustenance.
Those recollections to employ.
That bears no single dissonance,
just endless notes of joy.

So, let's enjoy each whisper,
each subtle offered word.
And, with smiles, administer,
each happy thought inferred.

Mike Hamill

The Rainbow Bridge

I lived a life of duty and joy.
Love, hugs, a special toy.
I had my humans who cherished me,
gave me hope and set me free.
My duty now is finally done.
I've served, I am a veteran, now gone.
So, don't be sad. Just look up.
There on the rainbow bridge; again pup.

Moonbeams And Raindrops

The moonbeams fall in soft profusion,
opalescent teardrops of confusion.
Shadows dance in a sublime display,
and drives the daytime far away.

Across the heavens the moon meanders,
as to the firmament it nightly panders.
Nyx drifts, in shadowy, spectral, form.
Chasing Selene through till dawn.

Raindrops fall with balletic grace,
slowly first but with increasing pace.
Swallowed at first by the waiting sand,
hidden, like stolen contraband.

And then into the earth it does coalesce,
drawn to Mother Gaia's breast.
There, life is given to the waiting seed,
upon which, the world will feed.

And now. Selene dips her head,
and Nyx follows in her stead.
And, to Helios, she bequeaths the sky.
As, another night falls from her eye.

Mike Hamill

Her Majesty's Farewell

I saw today, Her Majesty in repose.
Her guards surround her, in sentinel pose.
As she lay beneath her standard bright,
watched over through day and night.
The symbols of Monarchy above her lay,
as people together did come to pray.
They came in multitude, to stand before
Our Queen, in dignity and to honour.
To say farewell in thoughts and prayer.
To stand in supplication; foursquare!
Race, colour; nor creed was seen,
just sadness at the passing of our Queen!
Rest In Peace ma'am each heart will sing
As now we turn and cry. God Save The King!

My Garden & Other Poems

A Hebridean Sky

Beneath a Hebridean morning sky,
the dark clouds gather and scuttle by.
The snow falls in shimmering pearls of white.
And take the morning through till night.
The Eagle floats on each climbing draft,
that assemble in dances, choreographed.
Driven by the winds that race up the mountainsides,
and tumble back in roller coaster rides.
Oh, the Majesty, and the beauty in the eye,
as you travel through the Isle of Skye.

Mike Hamill

Icicles

Icicles form in the coldest sun
as translucent shapes they have begun.
In faded blues and emerald green
those colours that have always been
shaped in forms of icy flow
that glitter in the falling snow.
And shift their shapes, ere they begun
twixt wax and waning of moon and sun.

To blossom in the moons' cold shadow,
to drip from trees in meadows fallow.
Where avian troops in feathered cloaks
with whispered song do convoke.
Until the dawn, with creeping glide
draws pale sunlight to subside
upon ice sculptures, by night created.
To drip and fall. Until finally, dissipated.

Pathways

I wandered down a pathway, and
the subtle shades contained.
The route was forward and unplanned,
the destination ordained.

I saw a cloud of heavenly stars,
that glittered in my eyes.
And, like perfect exemplars,
the lake reflects the skies.

I heard a sound, the sweetest voice,
that rang in perfect pitch.
And all who hear the sound rejoice,
as harmonies bewitch.

I stumbled upon a field unshorn,
where gentle billows bring dancing fronds,
amongst a sea of ripening barleycorn.
To please this wandering vagabond.

The walk is endless, pleasures accruing.
The bounties are enjoyed.
The vistas all encompassing,
the senses; so, employed.

Mike Hamill

Broken Dreams

Another night of broken dreams,
of promises made but never redeemed.
Of treading paths repeatedly,
of hearing nightbirds sing to me

To watch the dawn through tired eyes.
And see the sun slowly rise.
To walk the house from door to door.
To wear my footprints on the floor!

Oh, these nights of broken dreams,
Are never ending, so it seems?
But light must come eventually,
And, no longer, each passing hour will I see

Another Winter's Tale

The winter sun fades to grey
and shortens with each passing day.
Leaves on trees, once bright and green,
fall dead and brown and lie unseen.

In wintry winds, the snowflakes play,
in natures organised disarray.
The shapes created do astound
their ethereal beauty does confound.

The fingers of Jack Frost explore,
icy tendrils to the fore.
Creating patterns on windowpanes
As winter dominance now gains.

The children, to the school now walk,
their breath misting as they talk.
Wrapped in cocoons of warming heat,
but still the cold nips at their feet.

As nighttime falls and the winds do blow,
the moonshine glistens on the earth below.
The birds in roosts now congregate,
as, for the morning warmth, they do wait

Mike Hamill

Winters Mist

I watch the mist at gentle play,
on meadowed fields as starts the day.
I see it trip and softly flow,
as morning breezes gently blow.
I see the dampness that it brings
and lie, glistening on gossamer wings
of butterflies in soft repose
amongst the thicket of hedgerows.

See the dawn now slowly rise
and the mist, with no compromise,
slowly fade till nought remains
amongst the endless grassy plains.
The meadow flower lifts up its head,
as cattle low and gently tread
amidst the damp and verdant field,
to see what treasures it does yield.

My Garden & Other Poems

Friends

A silent whisper drifts through the clouds
on shades of shining blue.
To walk eternally through my mind,
to remind me of you.
In azure dreams, I think of times,
to remember through the day.
And wander, in a somulent dream;
and watch the young at play.

I smile at things I see and hear
that comfort and enthral.
And sit, in embroidered symmetry,
beside a waterfall.
Is it either right or wrong
to search for truth out loud?
To be the shining metaphor
in the labyrinth of a crowd?

To talk of friends you've made or lost
through drifting shades of time.
To smile and think of them; in

Mike Hamill

meter and in rhyme?
To lay awake in happy tears.
As comes the morning new
And think of them most perfectly,
as acquaintances to renew.

Table For One

I sit alone on a sunlit beach, at a table just for one.
I watch the twilight fade away, at the setting of the sun.
I see the evening stars appear; luminescent shards of light,
twinkling in the skies above, beacons in the night.

I sit alone on a darkened beach at a table just for one.
And sift slowly through my memories, and savour each single one.
I see, in multicoloured frames of times and space.
I reminisce on each event; enjoying each remembered face.

I sit alone on a sandy beach at a table just for one
I smile at the warming, brought by the rising sun.
I look around, at the slowly gathering throng
and I am no longer alone. The loneliness is gone.

Mike Hamill

The Last Hurrah

My scribblings, for now exhausted. My work is complete.
The joy it brought me, as words did compete.
The thoughts and the meanderings of my mind
where, oft times neither were quite aligned!
I hope you've enjoyed these words of mine.
And return to them from time to time.
But now I close with this lasting thought.
Words are priceless, and their richness should be sought.

www.ingramcontent.com/pod-product-compliance
Lightning Source LLC
Chambersburg PA
CBHW072057110526
44590CB00018B/3209